# Introduction

If you enjoy knitting cozy afghans for your family and those you love, this collection offers varied designs that will work with many decorating styles.

We've included 15 patterns for scrap afghans, with the most lively and colorful designs we've seen! You will use a main color for the afghan and then enjoy adding a skein or less of each of many different colors.

Choose the four-color Subtle Chevron pattern to carry out a favorite decorating color scheme or choose the twenty-four color Rolling Ripple pattern to enliven any room! And while you enjoy brightening your environment, you'll be using up all that extra yarn at the same time!

# Afghan Directory

| Contents | Instructions | Color Photo |
|---|---|---|

# Rolling Ripple

## Skill Level:

EASY

## Size:
About 45 x 65 inches before fringe

## Materials:

 Medium (worsted weight) yarn, 12 oz (840 yds, 360 gms) Main Color (MC); 36 oz (2520 yds, 1080 gms) scraps

***Note:*** *Our photographed afghan was made with 12 oz (840 yds, 360 gms) green (MC) and 1½ oz (105 yds, 45 gms) each of 24 different colors.*

Size 10½ (6.5mm) 29-inch circular knitting needle

## Gauge:
In garter stitch (knit every row):
4 sts = 1 inch

## Instructions
With MC, cast on 180 sts.

**Row 1 (**right side**):**
Knit.

**Rows 2 and 3:**
Knit.

**Row 4:**
* (K2 tog tbl) twice; (YO, K1) 4 times; (K2 tog tbl) twice; rep from * across.

**Row 5:**
With any scrap color, knit.

**Rows 6 through 8:**
Rep Rows 2 through 4.

**Row 9:**
Knit.

**Rows 10 through 12:**
Rep Rows 2 through 4.

**Row 13:**
With MC, knit.

**Rows 14 through 16:**
Rep Rows 2 through 4.

Rep Rows 5 through 16, changing to new scrap color on each Row 5, until piece measures about 60 inches.

Rep Rows 5 through 15 once.

Bind off.

## Fringe
Following Fringe instructions on page 32, make Single Knot Fringe. Cut 18-inch strands of MC. For each knot use 2 strands. Tie knots evenly spaced (every other stitch) across each short end of afghan.

Trim ends even.

# Dashing Hues

## Skill Level:

EASY

## Size:
About 44 x 62 inches

## Materials:

Medium (worsted weight) yarn, 26 oz (1820 yds, 780 gms) Main Color (MC); 4 oz (280 yds, 120 gms) Color A; 10 oz (700 yds, 300 gms) scraps

*Note:* Our photographed afghan was made with 26 oz (1820 yds, 780 gms) off-white (MC), 4 oz (280 yds, 120 gms) blue (Color A), and 2 oz (140 yds, 60 gms) each of 5 different colors.

Size 8 (5mm) 29-inch circular knitting needle

## Gauge:
In stockinette st (knit one row, purl one row): 4 sts = 1 inch

## Instructions
*Notes: Slip all sts as to purl. Carry MC loosely along side edge when not in use.*

With MC, cast on 185 sts.

### Bottom Border
**Row 1 (**right side**):**
Knit.

**Rows 2 through 4:**
Rep Row 1.

### Body
**Row 1:**
With MC, knit.

**Row 2:**
Purl.

**Rows 3 and 4:**
Rep Rows 1 and 2.

**Row 5:**
With Color A, knit.

**Row 6:**
Knit.

**Rows 7 through 10:**
With MC, rep Rows 1 through 4.

**Row 11:**
With any scrap color, K1, sl 3; * K3, sl 1, K3, sl 3; rep from * to last st; K1.

**Row 12:**
K1, yf, sl 3, yb; * K3, yf, sl 1, yb, K3, yf, sl 3, yb; rep from * to last st; K1.

**Rows 13 and 14:**
With MC, rep Rows 1 and 2.

**Rows 15 and 16:**
With same scrap color, rep Rows 11 and 12.

**Rows 17 and 18:**
With MC, rep Rows 1 and 2.

**Rows 19 and 20:**
With same scrap color, rep Rows 11 and 12.

Rep Rows 1 through 20, changing to new scrap color on each Row 11, until afghan measures about 58 inches.

Rep Rows 1 through 10 once.

### Top Border
**Row 1 (**right side**):**
With MC, knit.

**Rows 2 through 5:**
Knit.

Bind off.

### Side Border
Hold afghan with right side facing you and one long side at top. With MC, pick up 220 sts evenly spaced along side.

**Row 1 (**wrong side**):**
Knit.

**Rows 2 through 4:**
Rep Row 1.

Bind off.

Repeat on other long side.

# Harmonious Stripes

**Skill Level:**

EASY

**Size:**
About 40 x 60 inches

**Materials:**

 Medium (worsted weight) yarn, 10 oz (700 yds, 300 gms) Main Color (MC); 42 oz (2940 yds, 1260 gms) scraps

***Note:*** *Our photographed afghan was made with 10 oz (700 yds, 300 gms) green (MC) and less than 3½ oz (245 yds, 105 gms) each of 14 different colors.*

Size 8 (5mm) 29-inch circular knitting needle

**Gauge:**
In stockinette st (knit one row, purl one row): 4 sts = 1 inch

## Instructions
With any scrap, cast on 181 sts.

### Bottom Border
**Row 1 (right side):**
Knit.

**Rows 2 through 4:**
Rep Row 1.

### Body
**Row 1 (right side):**
K1; * K5, P1; rep from * to last 6 sts; K6.

**Row 2:**
K1; * P5, K1; rep from * across.

**Rows 3 through 6:**
Rep Rows 1 and 2 twice more.

**Row 7:**
With MC, knit.

**Row 8:**
K1; * K5, P1; rep from * to last 6 sts; K6.

**Row 9:**
K1; * P5, K1; rep from * across.

**Rows 10 and 11:**
Rep Rows 8 and 9.

**Row 12:**
Rep Row 8.

**Row 13:**
With any scrap, knit.

**Row 14:**
K1; * P5, K1; rep from * across.

**Row 15:**
K1; * K5, P1; rep from * to last 6 sts; K6.

**Rows 16 and 17:**
Rep Rows 14 and 15.

**Row 18:**
Rep Row 14.

**Row 19:**
K1; * P5, K1; rep from * across.

**Row 20:**
K1; * K5, P1; rep from * to last 6 sts; K6.

**Rows 21 through 24:**
Rep Rows 19 and 20 twice.

**Rows 25 through 30:**
With same scrap, rep Rows 13 through 18.

Rep Rows 7 through 30 twelve times more.

Rep Rows 7 through 12 once.

With same scrap color as Row 1, rep Rows 13 through 18.

### Top Border
**Row 1:**
With same scrap color, knit.

**Rows 2 and 3:**
Rep Row 1.

Bind off.

# Woven Splendor

## Skill Level:

EASY

## Size:
About 40 x 55 inches before fringe

## Materials:
 Medium (worsted weight) yarn, 28 oz (1960 yds, 840 gms) Main Color (MC); 18 oz (1260 yds, 540 gms) scraps

**Note:** *Our photographed afghan was made with 28 oz (1960 yds, 840 gms) off-white (MC) and 1½ oz (105 yds, 45 gms) each of 12 different colors.*

Size 8 (5mm) 29-inch circular knitting needle

## Gauge:
In stockinette st (knit one row, purl one row):
4 sts = 1 inch

## Instructions
*Notes: Slip all sts as to purl. Carry MC loosely along side edge when not in use.*

With MC, cast on 184 sts.

## Bottom Border
**Row 1 (**right side**):**
Knit.

**Rows 2 through 4:**
Rep Row 1.

## Body
**Row 1:**
With MC, knit.

**Row 2:**
Purl.

**Row 3:**
With any scrap color, K4; * sl 2, K4; rep from * across.

**Row 4:**
K4; * yf, sl 2, yb, K4; rep from * across.

**Row 5:**
With MC, knit.

**Row 6:**
Purl.

**Row 7:**
With new scrap color, K1, sl 2; * K4, sl 2; rep from * to last st; K1.

**Row 8:**
K1, yf, sl 2, yb, K4; * yf, sl 2, yb, K4; rep from * to last 3 sts; sl 2, yb, K1.

Rep Rows 1 through 8 until afghan measures about 54 inches, ending by working a Row 2.

## Top Border
**Row 1:**
With MC, knit.

**Rows 2 through 5:**
Rep Row 1.

Bind off.

## Side Border
Hold afghan with right side facing you and one long side at top; with MC pick up 210 sts evenly spaced along side.

**Row 1:**
Knit

**Rows 2 through 4**
Rep Row 1.

Bind off.

Repeat on other long side.

## Fringe
Following Fringe instructions on page 32, make Single Knot Fringe. Cut 24-inch strands of MC. For each knot use 6 strands. Tie knots evenly spaced (every 4th stitch) across each short end of afghan. Trim ends even.

# Falling Leaves

## Skill Level:

INTERMEDIATE

## Size:
About 48 x 64 inches

## Materials:

Medium (worsted weight) yarn, 18 oz (1260 yds, 540 gms) Main Color (MC); 32 oz (2240 yds, 960 gms) scraps

*Note: Our photographed afghan was made with 18 oz (1260 yds, 540 gms) gray heather (MC) and 4 oz (280 yds, 120 gms) each of 8 different colors.*

Size 10 (5.75mm) 29-inch circular knitting needle

## Gauge:
In stockinette st (knit one row, purl one row): 4 sts = 1 inch

## Instructions
*Note: Slip all sts as to purl.*

With MC, cast on 181 sts.

### Bottom Border
**Row 1 (right side):**
Knit.

**Rows 2 and 3:**
Rep Row 1.

### Body
**Row 1 (wrong side):**
K4; purl to last 4 sts; K4.

**Row 2 (right side):**
Knit.

*Note: On following row, when working YOs, wrap yarn completely around the needle and back to front twice.*

**Row 3:**
K4, P3; YO twice; * P4, YO twice; rep from * to last 6 sts; P2, K4.

**Row 4:**
With any scrap color, K6; drop YOs, sl 1; * K1, insert right-hand needle in next st on 2nd row below st on needle, draw up lp, knit st on needle, pass lp over; K1, drop YOs, sl 1; rep from * to last 6 sts; K6.

**Row 5:**
K4, P2, sl 1; * P3, sl 1; rep from * to last 6 sts; P2, K4.

**Row 6:**
Knit.

**Row 7:**
K4, P3; YO twice; *P4, YO twice; rep from * to last 6 sts; P2, K4.

**Rows 8 through 35:**
Rep Rows 4 through 7 seven times more, changing to new scrap color on each Row 4.

**Row 36:**
With MC, rep Row 4.

**Row 37:**
Rep Row 5.

**Row 38:**
Knit.

**Row 39:**
K4; purl to last 4 sts; K3.

**Rows 40 through 53:**
Rep Rows 38 and 39 seven times more.

**Row 54:**
Knit.

**Row 55:**
Rep Row 3.

Rep Rows 4 through 55 four times more.

Rep Rows 4 through 39 once.

### Top Border
**Row 1:**
With MC, knit.

**Rows 2 and 3:**
Rep Row 1.

Bind off.

# Retro Ripple

## Skill Level:

EASY

## Size:
About 43 x 58 inches before fringe

## Materials:

Medium (worsted weight) yarn, 16 oz (1120 yds, 480 gms) Main Color (MC); 10 oz (700 yds, 300 gms) Color A; 20 oz (1400 yds, 600 gms) scraps.

*Note: Our photographed afghan was made with 16 oz (1120 yds, 480 gms) off-white (MC), 10 oz (700 yds, 300 gms) burgundy (Color A), and 2 oz (140 yds, 60 gms) each of 10 different scraps.*

Size 8 (5mm) 29-inch circular knitting needle

## Gauge:
In stockinette st (knit one row, purl one row): 4 sts = 1 inch

## Instructions

*Notes: Slip all sts as to knit. Do not carry unused colors.*

With MC, cast on 243 sts.

### Row 1 (right side):
K1, sl 1, K1, PSSO; K9, double dec (to work double dec: sl next 2 sts at the same time to right-hand needle, K1, P2SSO—double dec made); * K9, double dec; rep from * 17 times more; K9, K2 tog; K1.

### Row 2:
P6; double inc (to work double inc: purl next st leaving st on left-hand needle, YO, purl same st—double inc made); * P9; double inc; rep from * 18 times more; P6.

### Rows 3 through 12:
Rep Rows 1 and 2 five times more.

### Rows 13 through 16:
With Color A, rep Rows 1 and 2 twice.

### Rows 17 through 28:
With new scrap color, rep Rows 1 and 2 six times.

### Rows 29 through 32:
With Color A, rep Rows 1 and 2 twice.

### Rows 33 through 38:
With MC, rep Rows 1 and 2 three times.

Rep Rows 13 through 38 nine times more, changing to a new scrap color on each Row 17.

Rep Rows 13 through 16 once.

With MC, rep Rows 1 and 2 six times.

Bind off.

## Fringe
Following Fringe instructions on page 32, make Single Knot Fringe. Cut 24-inch strands of MC. For each knot use 5 strands. Tie knots evenly spaced (every increase and decrease) across each short end of afghan.

Trim ends even.

# Hyphenated Stripes

## Skill Level:

EASY

## Size:
About 44 x 62 inches

## Materials:
 Medium (worsted weight) yarn, 16 oz (1120 yds, 480 gms) Main Color (MC); 8 oz (560 yds, 240 gms) Color A; 15 oz (1050 yds, 450 gms) scraps.

*Note: Our photographed afghan was made 16 oz (1120 yds, 480 gms) green (MC), 8 oz (560 yds, 240 gms) yellow Color A, and less than 2½ oz (175 yds, 75 gms) each of 6 different colors.*

Size 8 (5mm) 29-inch circular knitting needle

Size H (5mm) crochet hook (for edgings)

## Gauge:
In stockinette st (knit one row, purl one row):
4 sts = 1 inch

## Instructions
*Notes: Slip all sts as to purl. Carry MC and Color A along side edge when not in use.*

With MC, cast on 183 sts.

### Bottom Border
**Row 1 (right side):**
Knit.

**Rows 2 through 4:**
Rep Row 1.

### Body
**Row 1 (right side):**
With MC, knit.

**Row 2:**
Purl.

**Row 3:**
With Color A, K1, sl 1; * K3, sl 1; rep from * to last st; K1.

**Row 4:**
K1, yf, sl 1, yb; * K3, yf, sl 1, yb; rep from * to last st; K1.

**Row 5 and 6:**
With MC, rep Rows 1 and 2.

**Row 7:**
With any scrap color, K3; * sl 1, K3; rep from * across.

**Row 8:**
K3; * yf, sl 1, yb, K3; rep from * across.

**Rows 9 and 10:**
With same scrap color, Rep Rows 7 and 8.

**Rows 11 through 60:**
Rep Rows 1 through 10, changing to new scrap color on Row 7.

Rep Rows 1 through 60 six times more.

Rep Rows 1 through 6 once.

### Top Border
**Row 1 (right side):**
With MC, knit.

**Rows 2 through 5:**
Rep Row 1.

Bind off.

### Side Edging
Hold afghan with right side facing you and one long side at top; with MC pick up 224 sts evenly spaced along side.

**Row 1 (wrong side):**
Knit.

**Rows 2 through 4:**
Rep Row 1.

Bind off.

Repeat on other long side.

### Fringe
Following Fringe instructions on page 32, make Single Knot Fringe. Cut 24-inch strands of MC. For each knot use 5 strands. Tie knots evenly spaced (every 5th stitch) across each short end of afghan. Trim ends even.

Dimensional Diamonds

Hyphenated Stripes

# Dimensional Diamonds

## Instructions

*Note: Slip all sts as to purl.*

With any scrap color, cast on 182 sts.

**Foundation Row:**
Purl.

**Row 1 (**right side**):**
With MC, knit.

**Row 2:**
K6; * yf, sl 2, yb, K6; rep from * across.

**Row 3:**
K6; * sl 2, K6; rep from * across.

**Row 4:**
Rep Row 2.

**Row 5:**
With any scrap color, K6; * sl 2, K6; rep from * across.

**Row 6:**
P6; * sl 2, P6; rep from * across.

**Rows 7 and 8:**
With same scrap color, Rep Rows 5 and 6.

**Row 9:**
With MC, knit.

**Row 10:**
K2, yf, sl 2 yb; * K6, yf, sl 2, yb; rep from * to last 2 sts; K2.

**Row 11:**
K2, sl 2; * K6, sl 2; rep from * to last 2 sts; K2.

**Row 12:**
Rep Row 10.

**Row 13:**
With new scrap color, K2, sl 2; * K6, sl 2; rep from * to last 2 sts; K2.

**Row 14:**
P2, sl 2; * P6, sl 2; rep from * to last 2 sts; P2.

**Rows 15 and 16:**
With same scrap color, rep Rows 13 and 14.

Rep Rows 1 through 16 until afghan measures about 50 inches.

**Next 4 Rows:**
Rep Rows 1 through 4.

**Next Row:**
With same scrap color as Foundation Row, knit.

Bind off.

## Side Edging

*Note: If not familiar with single crochet (sc) and reverse single crochet (reverse sc) stitches, refer to Crochet Edging page 31.*

Hold afghan with right side facing you and one long edge at top; with crochet hook and MC, make slip knot on hook and join with an sc in edge of first row in upper right-corner.

**Row 1:**
Working in ends of rows, work 225 sc evenly spaced across side. Ch 1, do not turn.

**Row 2:**
Working loosely, reverse sc in each sc.

Finish off.

Repeat on other long side.

## Fringe

Following Fringe instructions on page 32, make Single Knot Fringe. Cut 20-inch strands of MC. For each knot use 3 strands. Tie knots evenly spaced (every 3rd stitch) across each short end of afghan.

Trim ends even.

# Color Weave

## Skill Level:

EASY

## Size:
About 42 x 60 inches before fringe

## Materials:
 Medium (worsted weight) yarn, 28 oz (1960 yds, 840 gms) Main Color (MC); 20 oz (1400 yds, 600 gms) each of 8 different colors.

*Note:* Our photographed afghan was made with 28 oz (1960 yds, 840 gms) off-white (MC), and 2½ oz (175 yds, 75 gms) each of 8 different scraps.

Size 8 (5mm) 29-inch circular knitting needle

Size H (5mm) crochet hook (for edging)

## Gauge:
In stockinette st (knit one row, purl one row): 4 sts = 1 inch

## Instructions
*Notes: Slip all sts as to purl. Carry MC loosely along side edge when not in use.*

With MC, cast on 181 sts.

### Bottom Border
**Row 1 (right side):**
Knit.

**Rows 2 through 4:**
Rep Row 1.

**Row 6:**
Purl.

### Body
**Row 1 (right side):**
With any scrap color, K1, sl 3; * K5, sl 3; rep from * to last st; K1.

**Row 2:**
K1, yf, sl 3, yb; * K5, yf, sl 3, yb; rep from * to last st; K1.

**Row 3:**
With MC, K6, sl 1; * K7, sl 1; rep from * to last 6 sts; K6.

**Row 4:**
P6, sl 1; * P7, sl 1; rep from * to last 6 sts; P6.

**Rows 5 through 7:**
With same scrap color, rep Rows 1 through 3.

**Row 8:**
Purl.

**Row 9:**
With new scrap color, K5; * sl 3, K5; rep from * across.

**Row 10:**
K5; * yf, sl 3, yb, K5; rep from * to last 5 sts; K5.

**Row 11:**
With MC, K2, sl 1; * K7, sl 1; rep from * to last 2 sts; K2.

**Row 12:**
P2, sl 1; * P7, sl 1; rep from * to last 2 sts; P2.

**Rows 13 through 15:**
With same scrap color, rep Rows 9 through 11.

**Row 16:**
Purl.

Rep Rows 1 through 16 in sequence, changing to new scrap color on each Row 1 and on each Row 9, until afghan measures about 60 inches, ending by working a Row 8 or a Row 16.

### Top Border
**Row 1:**
With MC, purl.

**Rows 2 and 3:**
Rep Row 1.

Bind off as to purl.

### Side Edging
*Note: If not familiar with single crochet (sc) and reverse single crochet (reverse sc) stitches refer to Crochet Edging on page 31.*

Hold afghan with right side facing you and one long side at top; with crochet hook and MC, make slip knot on hook and join with an sc in edge of first row in upper right-hand corner.

**Row 1:**
Working in ends of rows, work 240 sc evenly spaced across side. Ch 1, do not turn.

**Row 2:**
Working loosely, reverse sc in each sc.

Finish off.

Repeat on other long side.

### Fringe
Following Fringe instructions on page 32, make Single Knot Fringe. Cut 24-inch strands of MC. For each knot use 6 strands. Tie knots evenly spaced (about every 4th stitch) across each short end of afghan.

Trim ends even.

Color Weave

Rainbow Ladder

# Rainbow Ladder

**Skill Level:**

**EASY**

**Size:**
About 42 x 60 inches before fringe

**Materials:**

Medium (worsted weight) yarn, 28 oz (1960 yds, 840 gms) Main Color (MC); 21 oz (1470 yds, 630 gms) scraps

*Note: Our photographed afghan was made with 28 oz (1960 yds, 840 gms) blue (MC) and 3 oz (210 yds, 90 gms) each of 7 different colors.*

Size 8 (5mm) 29-inch circular knitting needle

**Gauge:**
In stockinette st (knit one row, purl one row):
4 sts = 1 inch

## Instructions

*Notes: Slip all sts as to purl. Carry MC loosely along side edge when not in use.*

With MC, cast on 188 sts.

### Bottom Border
**Row 1 (**right side**):**
Knit.

**Rows 2 through 4:**
Rep Row 1.

### Body
**Row 1:**
With MC, knit.

**Row 2:**
Purl.

**Rows 3 and 4:**
Rep Rows 1 and 2.

**Row 5:**
With any scrap color, K8; * sl 2, K8; rep from * across.

**Row 6:**
K8; * yf, sl 2, yb, K8; rep from * across.

**Row 7:**
P8; * yb, sl 2, yf, P8; rep from * across.

**Row 8:**
Rep Row 6.

**Rows 9 through 12:**
Rep Rows 1 through 4.

**Rows 13 through 16:**
With new scrap color, rep Rows 5 through 8.

Rep Rows 1 through 8, changing to new scrap color on each Row 5, until afghan measures about 60 inches, ending by working a Row 4.

### Top Border
**Row 1 (**right side**):**
With MC, knit.

**Rows 2 through 5:**
Rep Row 1.

Bind off.

Weave in all ends.

### Fringe
Following Fringe instructions on page 32, make Single Knot Fringe. Cut 24-inch strands of MC. For each knot use 8 strands. Tie knots across each short end placing them at each at each blue stripe and at each end.

Trim ends even.

# California Sunset

**Size:**
About 44 x 60 inches before fringe

**Materials:**

Medium (worsted weight) yarn, 28 oz (1960 yds, 840 gms) Main Color (MC); 21 oz (1470 yds, 630 gms) scraps.

**Note:** *Our photographed afghan was made with 28 oz (1960 yds, 840 gms) lt purple (MC) and 3½ oz (245 yds, 105 gms) each of 6 different colors.*

Size 8 (5mm) 29-inch circular knitting needle

Size H (5mm) crochet hook (for edging)

**Gauge:**
In stockinette st (knit one row, purl one row):
4 sts = 1 inch

## Instructions

**Notes:** *Slip all sts as to purl. Carry MC loosely along side edge when not in use.*

With MC, cast on 182 sts.

**Row 1 (**right side**):**
Knit.

**Row 2:**
Purl.

**Rows 3 and 4:**
With any scrap color, knit.

**Row 5:**
With MC, K6; * sl 2, K6; rep from * across.

**Row 6:**
P6; * sl 2, P6; rep from * across.

**Row 7:**
With same scrap color, K6; * sl 2, K6; rep from * across.

**Row 8:**
Knit.

**Rows 9 and 10:**
With MC, rep Rows 1 and 2.

**Rows 11 and 12:**
With new scrap color, knit.

**Row 13:**
With MC, K2, sl 2; * K6, sl 2; rep from * to last 2 sts; K2.

**Row 14:**
P2, sl 2; * P6, sl 2; rep from * to last 2 sts; P2.

**Row 15:**
With same scrap color, K2, sl 2; * K6, sl 2; rep from * to last 2 sts; K2.

**Row 16:**
Knit.

Rep Rows 1 through 16 until afghan measures about 60 inches, ending by working a Row 2.

Knit one row.

Bind off as to purl.

## Border

**Note:** *If not familiar with single crochet (sc) stitch, refer to Crochet Edging on page 31.*

Hold afghan with right side facing you and one short side at top; with crochet hook and MC, make slip knot on hook and join with an sc in first row in upper right-hand corner.

**Rnd 1:**
2 sc in same sp as joining—beg corner made; working across side, sc in each st to last st; 3 sc in next st—corner made; working along next side in ends of rows, work 2 sc for every 3 rows to next side; working across next side, 3 sc in first st—corner made; sc in each st to last st; 3 sc in next st—corner made; working along next side in ends of rows, work same number of sc as on opposite side; join in joining sc.

**Rnd 2:**
Ch 1, sc in same sc as joining; 3 sc in next sc—corner made; * sc in each sc to 2nd sc of next corner; 3 sc in next sc; rep from * twice more; sc in each sc to first sc; join in first sc.

Finish off.

## Fringe

Following Fringe instructions on page 32, make Double Knot Fringe. Cut 24-inch strands of MC. For each knot use 6 strands. Tie knots evenly spaced (about every 5th stitch) across each short end of afghan.

Trim ends even.

# High-Flying Colors

**Skill Level:**

■■□□
EASY

**Size:**
About 44 x 60 inches before fringe

**Materials:**

**4** MEDIUM  Medium (worsted weight) yarn, 18 oz (1260 yds, 540 gms) Main Color (MC); 34 oz (2380 yds, 1020 gms) scraps.

*Note: Our photographed afghan was made with 12 oz (840 yds, 360 gms) off-white (MC), and 2½ oz (175 yds, 75 gms) each of 15 different colors.*

Size 9 (5.25mm) 29-inch circular knitting needle

**Gauge:**
In stockinette st (knit one row, purl one row):
9 sts = 2 inches

## Instructions

*Notes: Slip all sts as to purl. Do not carry unused colors.*

With MC, cast on 206 sts.

**Bottom Border**
**Row 1 (right side):**
Knit.

**Rows 2 through 4:**
Rep Row 1.

**Body**
**Row 1 (right side):**
With scrap color, K1; * sl 2, K4; rep from * to last st; K1.

**Row 2:**
P1, K2, P2; * sl 2, yb, K2, P2; rep from * to last 3 sts; sl 2, P1.

**Row 3:**
With new scrap color, K3, sl 2; * K4, sl 2; rep from * to last 3 sts; K3.

**Row 4:**
P3, sl 2, yb, K2; * P2, sl 2, yb, K2; rep from * to last st; P1.

**Row 5:**
With new scrap color, K5, sl 2; * K4, sl 2; rep from * to last st; K1.

**Row 6:**
P1; * sl 2, yb, K2, P2; rep from * to last st; P1.

**Rows 7 and 8:**
With MC, rep Rows 1 and 2.

**Rows 9 and 10:**
With new scrap color, rep Rows 3 and 4.

**Rows 11 and 12:**
With new scrap color, rep Rows 5 and 6.

**Rows 13 and 14:**
With new scrap color, rep Rows 1 and 2.

**Rows 15 and 16:**
With MC, rep Rows 3 and 4.

**Rows 17 and 18:**
With new scrap color, rep Rows 5 and 6.

**Rows 19 and 20:**
With new scrap color, rep Rows 1 and 2.

**Rows 21 and 22:**
With new scrap color, rep Rows 3 and 4.

**Rows 23 and 24:**
With MC, rep Rows 5 and 6.

Rep Rows 1 through 24 until afghan measures about 58 inches, ending by working any scrap color wrong side row.

**Top Border**
**Row 1:**
With MC, knit.

**Rows 2 and 3:**
Rep Row 1.

Bind off.

**Side Border**
Hold afghan with right side facing you and one long side at top; with MC, pick up 275 sts evenly spaced across side.

**Row 1:**
Knit.

**Rows 2 through 4:**
Rep Row 1.

Bind off.

Repeat on other long side.

**Fringe**
Following Fringe instructions on page 32, make Single Knot Fringe. Cut 24-inch strands of MC. For each knot use 4 strands. Tie knots evenly spaced (about every 4th stitch) across each short end of afghan.

Trim ends even.

# Streaked Stripes

**Size:**
About 44 x 60 inches

**Materials:**

 Medium (worsted weight) yarn, 18 oz (1260 yds, 540 gms) Main Color (MC); 27 oz (1890 yds, 810 gms) scraps.

***Note:*** *Our photographed afghan was made with 18 oz (1260 yds, 540 gms) variegated (MC), and 3 oz (210 yds, 90 gms) each of 9 different colors.*

Size 8 (5mm) 29-inch circular knitting needle

Size H (5mm) crochet hook (for edging)

**Gauge:**
In stockinette st (knit one row, purl one row):
4 sts = 1 inch

## Instructions

***Notes:*** *Slip all sts as to purl. Carry MC loosely along side edge when not in use.*

With any scrap color, cast on 185 sts.

**Row 1 (right side):**
Knit.

**Row 2:**
P1, K3; * P3, K3; rep from * to last st; P1.

**Row 3:**
With MC, K4, sl 3; * K3, sl 3; rep from * to last 4 sts; K4.

**Row 4:**
P1, K3; * yf, sl 3, yb, K3; rep from * to last st; P1.

**Rows 5 through 12:**
With same scrap color, rep Rows 1 through 4 twice more.

**Row 13:**
With new scrap color, knit.

**Row 14:**
P4, K3; * P3, K3; rep from * to last 4 sts; P4.

**Row 15:**
With MC, K1, sl 3; * K3, sl 3; rep from * to last st; K1.

**Row 16:**
P1, sl 3; * yb, K3, yf, sl 3; rep from * to last st; P1.

**Rows 17 through 24:**
With same scrap color, rep Rows 13 through 16 twice more.

Rep Rows 1 through 24 until afghan measures about 60 inches, ending by working a Row 12, or a Row 24.

**Next Row:**
With same scrap color, knit.

Bind off.

## Side Edging

***Note:*** *If not familiar with single crochet (sc) stitch, refer to Crochet Edging on page 31.*

Hold afghan with right side facing you and one short edge at top; with crochet hook and MC make slip knot on hook and join with an sc in first st, 2 sc in same sp as joining—beg corner made; working across edge, sc in each st to last st; 3 sc in next st—corner made; working along next side in ends of rows, work 2 sc for every 3 rows to next short edge; working across next edge, 3 sc in first st—corner made; sc in each st to last st; 3 sc in next st—corner made; working along next side in ends of rows, work same number of sc as on opposite side; join in joining sc.

Finish off.

# Subtle Chevron

**Size:**
About 40 x 54 inches

**Materials:**

 Medium (worsted weight) yarn, 21oz (1470 yds, 630 gms) Main Color (MC); 4 oz (280 yds, 120 gms) each Colors A and B; 14 oz (980 yds, 420 gms) scraps

***Note:*** *Our photographed afghan was made with 21 oz (1470 yds, 630 gms) off-white (MC), 4 oz (280 yds, 120 gms) each of green (Color A) and pink (Color B), and 3½ oz (245 yds, 105 gms) each of 4 different colors.*

Size 8 (5mm) knitting needles

**Gauge:**
In stockinette st (knit one row, purl one row):
4 sts = 1 inch

## Instructions

**Right-Hand Strip (make 1)**
With Color A, cast on 21 sts.

**Row 1 (right side):**
K4, (K2, P2) twice; K1, (P2, K2) twice.

**Row 2:**
P1, K2, P2, K2, P3, K2, P2, K2, P1, K4.

**Row 3:**
K5, P1, K2, P2, K5, P2, K2, P1, K1.

**Row 4:**
P3, K2, P2, K1, P1, K1, P2, K2, P3, K4.

Rep Rows 1 through 4 until strip measures about 54 inches, ending by working a Row 4.

Bind off.

**Left-hand Strip (make 1)**
With Color B, cast on 21 sts.

**Row 1 (right side):**
(K2, P2) twice; K1, (P2, K2) twice; K4.

**Row 2:**
K4, P1, K2, P2, K2, P3, K2, P2, K2, P1.

**Row 3:**
K1, P1, K2, P2, K5, P2, K2, P1, K5.

**Row 4:**
K4, P3, K2, P2, K1, P1, K1, P2, K2, P3.

Rep Rows 1 through 4 until strip has same number of repeats as Right-Hand Strip.

Bind off.

## Center Strips

**(make 5 MC strips and one strip of each of 4 scrap colors)**
Cast on 17 sts.

**Row 1:**
(K2, P2) twice; K1, (P2, K2) twice.

**Row 2:**
P1, K2, P2, K2, P3, K2, P2, K2, P1.

**Row 3:**
K1, P1, K2, P2, K5, P2, K2, P1, K1.

**Row 4:**
P3, K2, P2, K1, P1, K1, P2, K2, P3.

Rep Rows 1 through 4 until strip has same number of repeats as Right-Hand Strip.

Bind off.

## Assembly

Alternate MC and scrap color Center strips between Right-Hand and Left-Hand strips. Sew strips together.

## Fringe

Following Fringe instructions on page 32, make Single Knot Fringe. Cut 20-inch strands of MC. For each knot use 10 strands. Tie knots evenly spaced at each edge, each seam and in center of each strip across each short end of afghan.

Trim ends even.

# Watercolor Prism

## Size:
About 42 x 60 inches

## Materials:
 Medium (worsted weight) yarn, 6 oz (420 yds, 180 gms) Main Color (MC); 28 oz (1960 yds, 840 gms) scraps

**Note:** *Our photographed afghan was made with 6 oz (420 yds, 180 gms) It rose (MC), and less than 4 oz (280 yds, 120 gms) each of 8 different colors.*

Size 8 (5mm) 29-inch circular knitting needle

Size H (5mm) crochet hook (for edging)

## Gauge:
In stockinette st (knit one row, purl one row):
4 sts = 1 inch

## Instructions
**Note:** *Slip all sts as to purl, carry working color loosely behind slipped sts.*

With MC, cast on 182 sts.

## Bottom Border
**Row 1 (**right side**):**
Knit.

**Row 2:**
Knit.

## Body
**Row 1:**
Knit.

**Row 2:**
Purl.

**Row 3:**
With any scrap color, K2; * sl 4, K2; rep from * across.

**Row 4:**
P3, sl 2; * P4, sl 2; rep from * to last 3 sts; P3.

**Row 5:**
Knit.

**Row 6:**
Purl.

**Row 7:**
With new scrap color, K1, sl 2, K2; * sl 4, K2; rep from * to last 3 sts; sl 2, K1.

**Row 8:**
P1, sl 1, P4; * sl 2, P4; rep from * to last 2 sts; sl 1, P1.

**Rows 9 through 32:**
Rep Rows 1 through 8 three times more.

**Rows 33 and 34:**
Rep Rows 1 and 2.

**Rows 35 through 38:**
With MC, rep Rows 3 through 6.

**Rows 39 and 40:**
With first scrap color used, rep Rows 7 and 8.

Rep Rows 1 through 8 in color sequence as established until piece measures about 58 inches, ending by working a Row 2 or 6.

**Row 3 or 7:**
With MC, work in pattern across.

**Row 4 or 8:**
Work in pattern across.

**Row 5 or 1:**
Knit.

**Row 6 or 2:**
Purl.

## Top Border
**Row 1:**
Knit.

**Row 2:**
Knit.

Bind off.

## Edging
**Note:** *If not familiar with single crochet (sc) and reverse single crochet (reverse sc) stitches, refer to Crochet Edging on page 31.*

Hold afghan with right side facing you and one short edge at top; with crochet hook and MC, make slip knot on hook and join with an sc in first st.

**Rnd 1:**
2 sc in same sp as joining—beg corner made; working across edge, sc in each st to last st; 3 sc in next st—corner made; working along next side in ends of rows, work 2 sc for every 3 rows to next short edge; working across next edge, 3 sc in first st—corner made; sc in each st to last st; 3 sc in last st—corner made; working along next side in ends of rows, work same number of sc as on opposite side; join in joining sc.

**Rnd 2:**
Ch 1, working from left to right, reverse sc in each sc around, working 3 reverse sc in 2nd sc of each corner; join in first reverse sc.

Finish off.

# Abbreviations & Symbols

beg............................................... begin(ning)
dec....................................................decrease
K ...............................................................knit
K2 tog ................................... knit 2 together
P ................................................................ purl
P2 tog ................................... purl 2 together
patt........................................................ pattern
prev.................................................... previous
PSSO................... pass slipped stitch over
P2SSO.......... pass 2 slipped stitches over
rem ......................................... remain(ing)
rep ........................................... repeat(ing)
sk.................................................... skip
sl........................................................ slip
sl st(s) ................................. slip stitch(es)

sp(s)................................................. space(s)
st(s).............................................. stitch(es)
tbl................................ through back loop
tog...................................................... together
yb................................................. yarn in back
yf................................................. yarn in front
YO..................................................yarn over

\* An asterisk is used to mark the beginning of a portion of instructions to be worked more than once; thus, "rep from \* twice more" means after working the instructions once, repeat the instructions following the asterisk twice more (3 times in all).

† The dagger identifies a portion of instructions that will be repeated again later in the same row or round.

— The number after a long dash at the end of a row or round indicates the number of stitches you should have when the row or round has been completed.

() Parentheses are used to enclose instructions that should be worked the exact number of times specified immediately following the parentheses, such as "(K2, P2) twice."

[] Brackets and () parentheses are used to provide additional information to clarify instructions.

## Skill Levels for crochet

**BEGINNER**

Beginner projects for first-time knitters using basic stitches. Minimal shaping.

**EASY**

Easy projects using basic stitches, repetitive stitch patterns, simple color changes and simple shaping and finishing.

**INTERMEDIATE**

Intermediate projects with a variety of stitches, mid-level shaping and finishing.

**EXPERIENCED**

Experienced projects using advanced techniques and stitches, detailed shaping and refined finishing.

## Standard Yarn Weight System

Categories of yarn, gauge ranges, and recommended needle sizes

| Yarn Weight Symbol & Category Names | 1 SUPER FINE | 2 FINE | 3 LIGHT | 4 MEDIUM | 5 BULKY | 6 SUPER BULKY |
|---|---|---|---|---|---|---|
| Type of Yarns in Category | Sock, Fingering, Baby | Sport, Baby | DK, Light Worsted | Worsted, Afghan, Aran | Chunky, Craft, Rug | Bulky, Roving |
| Knit Gauge Range\* in Stockinette Stitch to 4 inches | 27–32 sts | 23–26 sts | 21–24 sts | 16–20 sts | 12–15 sts | 6–11 sts |
| Recommended Needle in Metric Size Range | 2.25–3.25 mm | 3.25–3.75 mm | 3.75–4.5 mm | 4.5–5.5 mm | 5.5–8 mm | 8 mm and larger |
| Recommended Needle U.S. Size Range | 1 to 3 | 3 to 5 | 5 to 7 | 7 to 9 | 9 to 11 | 11 and larger |

\* GUIDLINES ONLY: The above reflect the most commonly used gauges and needle or hook sizes for specific yarn categories.

### KNITTING NEEDLE CONVERSION CHART

| U.S. | 1 | 2 | 3 | 4 | 5 | 6 | 7 | 8 | 9 | 10 | 10½ | 11 | 13 | 15 | 17 | 19 | 35 | 50 |
|---|---|---|---|---|---|---|---|---|---|---|---|---|---|---|---|---|---|---|
| Continental-mm | 2.25 | 2.75 | 3.25 | 3.5 | 3.75 | 4 | 4.5 | 5 | 5.5 | 6 | 6.5 | 8 | 9 | 10 | 12.75 | 15 | 19 | 25 |

# Crochet Edging

## Single Crochet

Several of the afghans in this book have single crochet edgings.

Work a single crochet edging as follows.

**Step 1:**
With specified yarn, make a slip knot loop on crochet hook as shown in **Fig 1**.

**Fig 1**

**Step 2:**
To join with a single crochet stitch, with yarn at back of work, insert hook in stitch or space indicated from front to back (**Fig 2**).

**Fig 2**

Bring yarn over the hook from back to front and hook yarn (**Fig 3**).

**Fig 3**

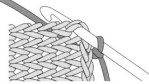

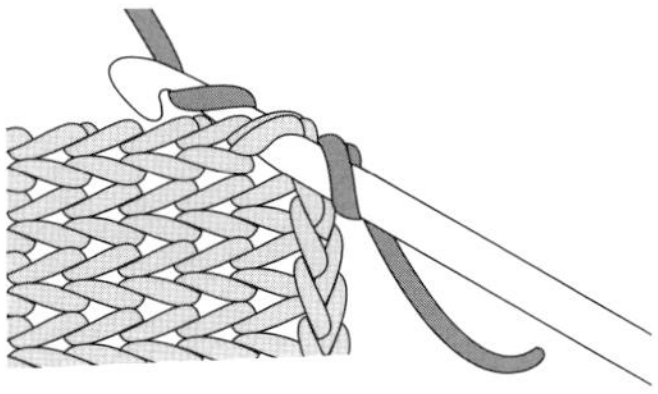

Draw yarn through stitch or space and up onto the hook. (2 loops on hook).

Again bring yarn over the hook from back to front, hook it and draw it through both loops on the hook (**Fig 4**).

**Fig 4**

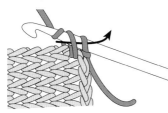

One loop will remain on the hook, and you have made one single crochet stitch (**Fig 5**).

**Fig 5**

**Step 3:**
To work additonal single crochet stitches, insert hook in next stitch or space, hook the yarn, draw it through, hook yarn again and draw it through both loops on hook—single crochet stitch made.

Continue working single crochet stitches as indicated in the specific pattern.

**Step 4:**
To work a second row of single crochet stitches, to chain 1. After completing the last single crochet stitch, bring yarn over the hook from back to front and hook it; draw hooked yarn through the loop on the hook and up onto the hook. You have now made one chain stitch (**Fig 6**).

**Fig 6**

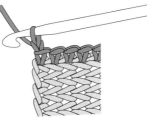

Now turn the work. Do not remove the hook from the loop as you do this.

Insert hook under both loops of the previous single crochet stitch as shown in **Fig 7**.

**Fig 7**

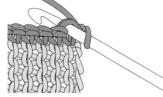

Work a single crochet stitch as before in each single crochet stitch to the end.

**Step 5:**
When working an edging around an afghan, it is necessary to join the last single crochet stitch made to the first one. To do this, insert hook under both loops of the first single crochet, hook yarn and draw it through stitch and through loop on hook. Now first and last single crochet stitches are joined.

## Reverse Single Crochet

Work from left to right, insert hook in st indicated (**Fig. 8**), draw lp through st— 2 lps on hook (**Fig. 9**); YO and draw through lps on hook.

**Fig 8**

**Fig 9**

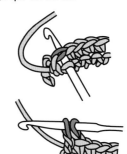

# Fringe Instructions

## Basic Instructions

Cut a piece of cardboard half as long as specified in instructions for strands plus ½" for trimming allowance. Wind yarn loosely and evenly lengthwise around cardboard. When card is filled, cut yarn across one end. Do this several times, then begin fringing; you can wind additional strands as you need them.

## Single Knot Fringe

Hold specified number of strands for one knot of fringe together, then fold in half. Hold afghan with right side facing you. Use crochet hook to draw folded end through space or stitch from right to wrong side (**Figs 1** and **2**), pull loose ends through folded section (**Fig 3**) and draw knot up firmly (**Fig 4**). Space knots as indicated in pattern instructions.

| Fig 1 | Fig 2 | Fig 3 | Fig 4 |
|---|---|---|---|

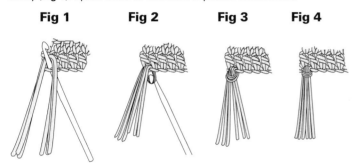

## Double Knot Fringe

Begin by working Single Knot Fringe completely across one end of afghan. With right side facing you and working from left to right, take half the strands of one knot and half the strands in the knot next to it, and knot them together (**Fig 5**).

**Fig 5**

## Triple Knot Fringe

First work Double Knot Fringe. Then working again on the right side from left to right, tie third row of knots as in **Fig 6**.

**Fig 6**

Patterns tested and models made by Tammy Hebert, Carol Mansfield, Nel Sanchez, Sandy Scoville, Sue Steele, Barbara Tritchler and Kathy Wesley.

**American School of Needlework** ®
excellence in instruction

2420 Grand Avenue, Suite H
Vista, California 92081

www.ASNpub.com

©2004 by American School of Needlework, Inc.

The full line of ASN products is carried by Annie's Attic catalog.

**TOLL FREE ORDER LINE** or to request a free catalog (800) 582-6643

**Customer Service** (800) 282-6643, **Fax** (800) 882-6643

Visit www.AnniesAttic.com

ISBN: 978-1-59012-069-9    All rights reserved.    Printed in U.S.A.        8 9